THROUGH THE EYES OF

JESUS

THROUGH THE EYES OF

JESUS

MACK THOMAS

Illustrated by Hilber Nelson

GOLD 'N' HONEY FAMILY CLASSICS

"But we have the mind of Christ."

1 CORINTHIANS 2:16

THROUGH THE EYES OF JESUS

published by Gold'n'Honey Books
a part of the Questar publishing family

© 1995 by Questar Publishers, Inc.
Illustrations © 1995 by Hilber Nelson
Designed by David Uttley

International Standard Book Number: 0-88070-803-4

Printed in Mexico

For information:
Questar Publishers, Inc., Post Office Box 1720
Sisters, Oregon 97759

95 96 97 98 99 00 01 02 — 10 9 8 7 6 5 4 3 2 1

Contents

Introduction

Just imagine,

on some starry night, that you're in a sailing ship high in

God's heavens, traveling from galaxy to galaxy in the ocean of the universe.

Jesus is with you.

He shows you how to set the sails. He lets you try it by yourself.

Then the two of you stand together in the ship's bow, and watch.

Stars and comets pass quickly by on both sides.

You decide that here in the heavens, the word *starboard* fits better

as the name for a ship's right side than it did on earth.

Earth. Ah, yes. It seems so far away.

But once there was a time when you lived there.

And you know that once there was a time when Jesus did too.

You wonder what those days were like for him. What did he enjoy looking at?

What did he like to listen to? What smells and tastes does he remember?

What did he touch and feel? What made him laugh?

What made him cry?

What was he always thinking about and praying about?

Jesus knows what's on your mind.

"Would you like me to tell you about it?" he asks.

His voice is warm and deep.

Yes, you really would.

He leans forward with his hands folded and his elbows on the rail.

You see silver starshine reflected in his eyes as he begins speaking.

And the story goes something like this...

So Much to Tell

ONE DAY when I was a little boy, I came running into our family's carpentry shop. I squatted on the packed-dirt floor, and picked up sawdust and shavings. I rubbed them hard between my palms, then cupped my hands close to my face. I liked the smell of wood.

My nose also caught the welcome aroma of my mother's lentil soup cooking slowly on a low fire in our house next door. My mouth watered. It was one of my favorite meals. I said a prayer of thanksgiving for my mother's skill.

She was seated outside in the narrow space between the shop and the house. The midday sun gave a gleam to her white linen head-covering. She was sewing a new cloak for her growing son to wear. I saw her lay her needle down, and rise, and step inside to tend the soup.

I had just finished my outdoor chores. But here in the shop there might be more work. When the time was right, I could sweep up these shavings and sawdust to leave the floor clean. But maybe there was more I could do first.

In the middle of the shop floor, Joseph was drilling holes in a beam. He wore a woodchip in his ear, which was the proud sign to everyone that he was a carpenter.

"Can I help you?" I asked.

"Thank you, Jesus," he answered. He motioned me closer. "I'm nearly finished with this yoke. Here, feel it." Joseph stopped drilling. He softly stroked the beam that soon would rest on the shoulders of two oxen pulling a plow.

I put my hand next to Joseph's, which was more than twice as large as mine. I slid my fingers along the smoothness of the wood.

He reached under and lifted the beam a few inches. "And it's light," he said. "Strong, but light. Easy for oxen to bear. So they can serve their master better than ever." I gave thanks to God in heaven for Joseph's skill.

He took up the drill again, and winked at me. "And someday, I expect you'll make even lighter and easier yokes than this one," he whispered.

Mary stepped into the sunshine again. She called softly: "Joseph, we can eat whenever you like." She leaned over to pick up the new cloak.

"Thank you, Mary," Joseph answered. He set the drill aside. He leaned back with his hands against the floor. He stretched his bare legs and feet on the dirt toward the doorway. He said to me, "But before we clean up, tell me the Scripture you heard at the synagogue yesterday."

I leaned back the same way Joseph did. I recited a passage from the scroll of the prophet Isaiah. It began like this: "For unto us a child is born, unto us a son is given, and the government will be on his shoulder...." I remembered it easily. I'd been thinking about this passage, just as I did each week with every Scripture I heard on the Sabbath Day in the synagogue. I never forgot them. To me, God's words belonged inside me, just as much as the breaths I took or the beating of my heart. I always heard them sounding in my head in a deep, peaceful voice. It was a familiar voice that never sounded strange or new.

I saw the pleasure on my parents' faces when I quoted the passage perfectly. I pulled my knees to my chest and locked my arms around them. I asked Joseph, "This child that Isaiah tells about — do you know who he is?"

Joseph's smile faded. I saw a startled expression on Mary's face as well. She stepped inside, and knelt next to Joseph. Between her folded hands she held the new cloak. "Perhaps this is the time to tell him," she said to her husband. They were on one side of the new yoke, with me on the other.

"My son," Mary began. "When God chose to bring you into the world, he sent an angel to tell me. The angel said I was to have a baby, a son, to be named Jesus."

She tightened her grip on the cloak as she continued. "And the angel said, 'He will be great. He will be called the Son of the Most High. The Lord God will give him the throne of King David. He will reign forever, and his kingdom will never end....'"

As I listened, I heard not only my mother's voice, but also the same familiar voice I always heard in Scripture. I liked how they sounded together.

I reached out again to rub the fresh smoothness of the yoke. I looked up at Mary. "Were you happy to let God do this for you?"

She relaxed her grip on the cloak. She smiled. "Yes, Jesus. I told the angel, 'I am the servant of the Lord. May everything you say truly happen to me.' And so far, Jesus, everything has happened exactly as the angel said."

"Is there more you can tell me?" I asked.

Joseph grinned, and put his arm around Mary. "Plenty more!" he said. "An angel also spoke to me, Jesus, in a dream. And we have gifts to show you from wise men who traveled far to find you. And God lit a new star to guide them. And on the night you were born there came an army of angels! And — oh, Jesus, there's so much more to tell you. Let's get up from this floor, and we'll talk about it while we eat."

Joseph helped Mary to stand. She stepped across to pour up the soup.

Joseph put away his tools.

The time was right, so I quickly swept up the shavings and sawdust from Joseph's work, leaving the shop floor clean.

An Offering

I HARDLY NOTICED the tiredness burning in the soles of my feet. I was too excited. At last we were here in Jerusalem, after a three days' journey on foot.

I was twelve — the age when boys in Israel could be called "sons of the law." They had been taught the Scriptures; now they were expected to obey whatever God's law said. Now I was old enough to be a part of everything at this year's Passover, the greatest and oldest festival which God's law required.

I looked up at the temple's golden face. It reached nearer to heaven than any building I'd ever seen. Doves flew around the towering pillars. Bending my head to look higher, I felt the skin wrinkle in the back of my neck.

All around Joseph and me were husbands and fathers and older sons from all over Israel. Like us, they came to the temple to get a slaughtered lamb for tonight's Passover meal with their family. While waiting, they chanted verses from the Psalms. The thousands of voices made a rumbling hum that never stopped. I, too, called aloud a verse: "I was glad when they said to me, Let us go to the house of the Lord!" Even in Nazareth I'd never felt so much at home as I did now.

I closed my eyes and took a deep breath. I caught the pleasing smell of roasting fat blazing on the great altar not far away. The fat had been cut away from lambs being killed by the hundreds on this holy day. Now it was burning as an offering to God.

Gazing at the clouds above the temple, I remembered the law's words: *a burnt offering, an offering made by fire, an aroma pleasing to the Lord.*

Animals were sacrificed every day at the temple. Thousands of lambs and bulls and goats and birds were offered year by year. But how could their death be enough to please God? All those sacrifices could never take away everybody's sin. How could any animal take the place of a human being? Men and women and boys and girls were made in God's image. Animals were not.

No. There had to be another sacrifice.

Suddenly, another Scripture passage echoed in my mind. The rabbi in Nazareth had read this verse from the scroll. It was from the Second Psalm: *You are my Son; today I have become your Father.* I heard the words not in the rabbi's voice, but in the older, deeper voice I always heard in God's law. I listened again: *You are my Son... You are my Son... You are my Son....*

Again I looked into the sky and prayed: *Thank you, my Father, for your love for me!* Yes, the Scriptures were my Father's loving words, this temple was my Father's earthly house, and I was my Father's only Son.

The crowd kept chanting.

I remembered another Scripture. I called out the words of Psalm Forty:

> *You prepared a body for me. And I said, "Here I am!*
> *It's written about me in the scroll. I have come to do your will, O God.*
> *Your law is inside my heart."*

I prayed again. *Thank you, Father, for this body you prepared for me. I give it to you. With it, I will make the perfect sacrifice. Yes, O God — I will do your will!*

I raised my arms. The doves flew low, and passed right above me. Then they quickly flew up again to circle the golden temple.

The Beginning

T THE EDGE of the River Jordan, I slipped off my sandals and stepped in. I felt cool water at my ankles, then around my knees, then at my thighs.

Today I would start the work my Father sent me here to do. My childhood was over, and so were my days as a growing young man. This was the real beginning. Starting now, every moment of my life would paint a picture for all to see. I would show the world what it means to live as God's child.

John the Baptizer was waiting for me. I knelt before him. The river swirled to my chest.

He responded as I expected: *"I* should be baptized by *you!* Why do you come to me?"

"Let it be this way today," I answered. "This is how we can bring about what God says is right." I folded my arms across my chest. I bowed my head, and closed my eyes.

I felt John's strong hand at the back of my head. His other hand gripped my folded arms. I relaxed completely. Slowly, gently, John slipped me back under the water's surface.

The river rolled over my face and my folded arms. Holding my breath, I had time to count to three. I thought of Jonah, under water three days in a fish's belly.

I felt John lifting me. Up from the river I arose. With water dripping from my elbows and beard and shoulders, I prayed: *Father, keep showing me what you want me to do. And give me the strength to do it every day.*

I lifted my eyes to the sky, as I always loved to do. Never on earth had I seen what I saw now. In one place the blue rolled back. Through the opening I saw the light of my home in heaven. It was golden light, richer in color and more dazzling than the sun. In the center of the light, far inside the opening, I saw the Holy Spirit coming toward me. But when the Spirit reached the opening and stepped out into the blue, he changed into the form of a dove. The dove flew downward, while behind him the blue closed up. The golden light went away.

As the dove glided closer, I leaned my head back. I held out my arms. The dove landed on my chest and disappeared. I breathed deeply, and felt a strength I had never known.

Again I heard the voice that always sounded in my heart when the Scriptures were read. This time, however, my Father was speaking aloud — as loud as a strong wind or a roaring fire. "I love you!" he called. "You're my beloved Son. In you I take great delight!"

Every son longs to hear those words from his father. I heard them from mine, and I was glad.

Not by Bread

I STOOD FOR A MOMENT to enjoy the sunset my Father was painting. My body was weak from tiredness and lack of food. I couldn't stay long on my feet. I sat again. I picked up a rock, and held it.

I called out a verse from the Psalms: "Praise to the Lord my Rock, who trains my hands for war, and my fingers for battle!"

Then I saw movement in the dark shadows of the ravine in front of me. The meeting I had been expecting was about to begin: Satan was moving in.

This was why the Spirit guided me to the desert. He led me straight here from the River Jordan, where forty days ago John baptized me. For forty days and nights I had seen no human being. Nor had I tasted a single bite of food.

All this time I had been praying. Again and again I thought through the entire Scriptures word by word, line by line. In every passage I heard my Father's voice of wisdom. In every book I saw his plan for his Son. He was training me for my work. His words were the food I craved.

Every hour of every day and night, Satan and his demons lingered on the hills nearby. They howled. They screamed and cursed. Each time I bowed my head or looked up at the sky or spoke a passage of Scripture, their ugly voices blared. This was not a vacation I had come to. It was a battle.

Now Satan was ready to attack. His moment had come. He was determined to overcome me as he had overcome Adam.

The rock was still in my hand. God's word was in my heart: *You, O Lord, are my rock and my helper...*

I knew what was coming. I prayed aloud: "O Father, your enemy Satan has come to offer me bread and more. I know he only wants me to turn my back on you, and go against your plan. He wants me to disobey you. He knows that if I sin even once, my punishment must be death. He wants me dead, so he can torment me in hell forever. He knows that if he defeats me, he has won the final battle. He will have defeated God.

"But I will listen only to you, my Father. I'm your Son and I'm like you in every way. You've also made me a man, and I'm like man in every way. You'll let me be tempted in every way. But, Father, I will not sin. I choose to obey you. I'll depend on you in every way a man should, so I can show my brothers and sisters how to trust you.

"Dear Father, let the words of my mouth and the thoughts of my heart be pleasing to you.

Give me your answer to everything Satan says."

Suddenly I noticed that the demons had hushed for the first time in nearly six weeks. Satan had taken the form of a shadow. I saw him sliding closer. The shadow fill the ravine. It flowed up to cover the dry, rocky slope on each side.

I would not stop him. I stood, and took a step forward.

He let the quietness settle in. Then he broke it: "Since you're the Son of God," he said smoothly, "tell that rock to become a loaf of bread."

For forty days, I hadn't even wanted to eat. I had filled my heart and soul and body and mind with Scripture. But now, with my Father's permission, the enemy threw thoughts of fresh bread at me, like flaming darts. I could smell fresh bread. I remembered the taste of fresh bread. My mouth watered. My tongue and my hollow stomach and even my hands and fingers were gripped by hunger. My nerves and muscles demanded bread — *now*. My body cried out that it would die if I didn't feed it.

But I would not. I would work no miracle to serve only myself. I would use my power only to do what my Father told me, even if I must die.

I heard my Father's voice. I called out the words to rebuke Satan's challenge: "Scripture says that man doesn't live by bread alone, but by every word that comes from God's mouth."

I turned my back on Satan, and faced the western sky. The sun was gone. The evening had begun. I knew he had more temptations to throw at me, even tonight. And sooner or later, before my life on earth was over, he would come after me with every weapon he had.

Yes, life on earth was a battle. I would be bloody and bruised before the end. But this was what my Father had trained me for. And I would not sin.

I tossed the rock from hand to hand, and prayed: *My Father, your will be done on earth as it is in heaven...*

Joy

T HE SURPRISED SERVANTS poured the new wine from jar to pitcher and from pitcher to cup. Only a moment before, this sparkling red liquid had been ordinary water, clear and tasteless. With only a word, and with only the servants and a few others watching, I turned the water into wine. Instantly I made more than a hundred gallons, enough to keep this wedding feast going for days.

As the drink was served and sipped and sipped again, the guests laughed and sang and danced more freely. The musicians played faster. Everyone's face had a smile. I clapped my hands and tapped my toes. This was like the joy my Father wanted everyone to have forever.

I thought of another wedding feast, still to come. It would take place in heaven, and the singing and dancing and celebrating would last forever. I myself would be the bridegroom, and all my people would be the bride. The happiness at today's wedding could only be a small picture of this happy feast in the future.

I mingled among the merrymakers. I saw a man step up to the bridegroom. "My compliments!" he remarked. "Most people serve their best refreshment first, but you saved it for last!"

A servant with a pitcher passed close to me. I put one hand on his shoulder and another on the pitcher. "May I help you serve?" I asked. He was reluctant to let a guest perform a servant's duties, but I assured him it was my pleasure.

Carrying the pitcher, I made my way through the crowd to where some of my newly chosen disciples were standing: Peter and Andrew, James and John, and Philip and Nathaniel. They, too, had witnessed what I did to the water. But they were still staring at me in wonder, hardly able to believe what they had seen.

Into each of their cups I poured a generous portion of the new wine. They sipped it cautiously at first. Then each man's lips and mouth and tongue convinced him that his eyes were not mistaken. This wasn't water anymore! It was a fresh creation. The old was gone, and the new had come.

I poured myself a cup as well. As we enjoyed my new creation together, I saw in my disciples' eyes that they were learning to trust me.

In the Dark

NICODEMUS NEEDED TIME to think. So before I told him anything more, I looked away. This was the evening hour when children all across Jerusalem were saying bedtime prayers. On a rooftop I saw a boy point at a shooting star that my Father and I had made just for tonight.

The boy didn't see where it came from, or where it went. But he was delighted by it, and it gave him something special to be thankful for in his prayers.

Nicodemus hadn't noticed any stars tonight. When he first entered this courtyard, his head was down. He was carrying a lamp. He guarded the flame with his cupped hand so the breeze wouldn't blow it out. He greeted me and set the lamp on the ledge beside him. He thought the courtyard walls would protect the flame from the evening breeze.

He was a famous teacher. Everyone in Jerusalem knew of him. But I knew Nicodemus better than they did. I knew how much he wanted to know God and see God. I knew he was an old man who wanted to be young inside forever, but didn't know how.

Now was the time to teach the teacher.

I told Nicodemus he needed to be born all over again. I looked into the sky and I said, "You must be born from above." Nicodemus didn't understand. "How?" he asked, as the slightest breeze entered the courtyard. It barely tossed the white, wispy ends of his beard.

"I tell you the honest truth," I answered, "you must be born by the Spirit." Nicodemus did not understand this either. He needed time to think.

Suddenly a stronger breeze blew across the courtyard. Nicodemus remembered his lamp. Too late, he reached for it on the ledge. The flame flickered and bent, then sputtered out. He turned back to me with an irritated look.

"The wind blows wherever it wants to," I said, stretching my hand and feeling the breeze through my fingers. "You hear the sound. But you don't know where it comes from, or where it's going. That's exactly how it is with God's Holy Spirit."

Nicodemus bent forward. "But *how?*" he pleaded.

"You're a famous teacher," I said, "and yet you don't understand these simple things?"

I silently prayed, *My Father, help Nicodemus know that your ways are like the wind, which no man can measure and pour. Help him wait for you. Help him watch for your Spirit.*

I gave Nicodemus more time to think. Finally he folded his hands and pressed them against his hairy chin. Then he looked up, just as another shooting star left a trail. His prayer was short and silent, but I heard it. He asked my Father to help him understand.

Flowers of the Field

⚬⚬⚬

AFTER CLIMBING from the lakeshore, I stopped halfway up the hill. I sat down where my Father had decorated the mountain grass with wildflowers — pale yellow rock-roses, tiny blue windflowers, and mountain lilies as richly purple as a king's robe. I watched the crowd climbing after me. They gathered around, waiting and listening.

All morning by the lakeshore, I had been healing these people. I wrapped my hands around

crippled arms and legs. I rubbed the throats of those who were coughing, and held my fist against their aching chests. I soothingly stroked the skin of those who were covered with sores. I touched deaf ears to make them hear, and blind eyes to make them see. There were others whose shoulders I gripped as I commanded demons to come out of their bodies.

And everyone I touched that morning was healed.

One brown-eyed girl came to me with a face wrinkled by pain and trouble. She lowered her head, as if she were ashamed to look at me. All she wore was a tunic. It was torn on one shoulder, and had holes near the neck.

I pressed my palms to her face. Her soft skin was fearfully hot with fever. With a lighter touch, I slowly slid two fingers down her temple, then her cheek. I let my fingers rest just a moment on her chin.

At once I saw her relief. The fever was gone. Most of the wrinkles on her forehead were gone as well.

But she didn't smile. She put her hand on her shoulder where the tunic was torn. Her eyes asked for more.

But the others around her had grown noisier and pushier. They were hungry for their turn to be healed. The crowd seemed to swallow her up, forcing her back and away, out of my sight until I could find her again.

And just now I found her. Not far to my left, she was by herself, seated on the grass.

I looked around at my listeners. And I began to teach: "How happy are the poor in spirit, for the kingdom of heaven is theirs. How happy are those who cry in grief and sorrow, for they will be comforted...."

As I spoke, I glanced often at the girl sitting alone and unsmiling. She was hearing my every word. I called out, "Take a look at the flowers of the field!" I swept my arm wide toward the blooms all around.

She turned. Close to her elbow she saw a small lily, as if for the first time. It had one purple bloom.

"See how they grow?" I asked. "They never work or sew to make what they wear. But see how richly God dresses them! I tell you, not even King Solomon in his best royal robes was ever dressed this well!"

I saw the girl reach out to pick the lily. She brought the flower close. She slowly twirled it in her fingers, as I continued in a loud voice: "So why worry about clothes, you people of little faith?"

At these words, she let go of the flower.

I stared straight at her, and smiled. My voice was gentler now. "If this is how God dresses the wild grass on a mountainside, won't he even more richly take care of you?"

Her face reddened. She stayed completely still as I continued teaching.

"So don't worry," I said, "about what to eat or what to drink or what to wear. People who don't love God always rush after these things. But your heavenly Father knows exactly what you need. So go after what *God* wants. Go after what *he* says is right."

I saw the girl take up the flower again. She carefully arranged the blossom in one of the holes near the neck of her tunic. Then she held her head high to watch me and listen.

On her face was the first smile she had worn all day.

Safe in the Storm

T HE SCREAMING WIND and troubled waves did not wake me. The shouts of my disciples did. These were the men my Father gave me. They were my friends, my chosen brothers.

And they were afraid.

Earlier this evening, when we first settled into the boat, I was tired. I told the men to cross to the other side of the lake, while I rested here in the back. I lay down and closed my eyes. My mind was cheered by this promise from Scripture: *I will lie down and sleep in peace, for you alone, O Lord, keep me safe.*

Now I opened my eyes. The gray, stormy sky gave just enough evening light for me to see the fear in these men's faces. The sight saddened me, because it was so unnecessary.

"Master!" Andrew cried, "we're about to die!"

I ran my hand through my hair and beard. I felt the wetness from the spray coming off the waves. The boat was rocking and heaving. I gripped the side of the boat.

Father, I prayed, *thank you for Andrew. Thank you that he is NOT about to die. I am with him, I am life, and we will cross to the other side, just as I told him.*

Behind Andrew, I saw James wrestling with an oar that pitched wildly. The waves were stronger than even James's powerful arms. He stole a quick, desperate glance at me. He screamed: "Lord, save us!"

The boat rose and fell and rose again. I thanked God that James wanted my help. *Father, help him learn to seek my help even when he isn't afraid.*

Philip also looked back, his arms wrapped around the mast. Seeing me awake, he yelled above the storm's fury: "Teacher, don't you even care if we drown?"

My Father, I prayed, *help all these men realize that your own Son is aboard this boat. Help them remember that this is your mission we are on, in the middle of the Sea of Galilee. Help my brothers understand that tonight this boat is unsinkable. Help them throw all their worrisome fear on me, because I care for them.*

Someday these men would be fearless in the face of far worse storms than this. Someday they would realize that riding out a storm makes a man stronger than ever, more alive than ever. Someday they would know. Tonight, they did not.

I sat up. I called aloud, so all of my men could hear: "Your faith is so small! *Why* are you so afraid?"

Each man stared at me, but not one could answer my question. Their fear was too strong to let them think clearly.

A fierce new blast of wind tore at us, slapping our faces with spray from the sea.

The boat jerked wildly to one side. The men crashed into one another. I heard Peter scream.

Their fear of death was everything now. They had forgotten how often I spoke to them about the work they must do in the future. They had forgotten that I myself had unfinished work on earth to do. They didn't realize that this storm was like every storm. My Father sent the wind and the waves to help train them for their earthly work — not to steal them away from it.

I stood. I set my feet wide apart, to steady myself in the lurching boat. Staring into the angry storm, I stretched out my hand. "Peace!" I ordered. "Be still!"

At once it was over.

The rising moon burst through a break in the clouds. The air was still. The water was calm. The rocking of the boat became a gentle swaying motion, then died away.

Everything was quiet.

It happened so fast that the moonlight showed James still clutching the oar as if it meant to fly away. Philip's arms were still locked around the mast.

Now they could think. "Tell me," I asked them: "Why didn't you trust me? Why do you have such little faith?"

No Fear

I N ALL HER LIFE she had never seen the face looking over her now.
But she wasn't afraid of me.

For the last hour she had been away from this life. Her spirit had gone to where the things of this earth fade away. The path she took was shadowy, but she had also seen the beginning of true light, beautiful light. And she had heard a voice. The light and the voice kept her from being afraid.

Now, waking up from this sleep of death, she saw in my eyes that same light. That was why she still wasn't afraid.

I held her face in my hands. I repeated the words I spoke to bring her back into this world: "Young girl, get up."

The surprise in her eyes told me she recognized my voice. She raised up on her elbows, and gazed into my eyes. I knew the questions racing in her mind: Who was I? Why did I seem so familiar? Had she been dreaming about me?

A sniffle behind me made her notice the others in the room. In the corner were my disciples Peter and James and John, more new faces staring at her. Peter was wiping a tear from his eye. Next to them she saw her mother and father, who also looked ready to burst into cries of joy. She quickly got up and ran into their arms.

Someone was wailing outside. The girl stepped to the window, and saw the crowd of neighbors gathered to weep in front of her house. She turned to her father. "Why are they here? What are they doing?"

Her father struggled to explain. "They — We — You were so sick. And they were afraid you had died."

She stepped back to her parents. "And you, Father: Were you afraid?"

As he embraced his daughter, he looked at me. "I was afraid — yes, my child, I was. Until the Master told me not to be. He told me just to believe him. So I did."

The girl needed no more explanation. She frowned, and put her hands on her stomach.

"She's hungry," I said to her parents. "Can you get her something to eat?"

They walked with her out of the room. And I prayed: *Thank you, Father, for sending me here to destroy the fear of death.*

No Turning Back

STRETCHED MY LEGS, and watched my disciples. They had finished a good meal with me, though two last fish were still roasting on the fire. The men were resting and talking and thinking.

This morning, on the road here, I had asked them, "Who do you think I am?" Peter answered for everyone: "You are the Son of the living God."

I blessed Peter for his answer. He was learning to listen to God, and God had given him those words. I told Peter and all of them that I was giving them the keys to my Father's kingdom.

Now, as they relaxed by the lakeshore, I knew what they were wondering: If I, their leader, was setting up a kingdom, what rewards and privileges would that mean for them?

Peter came and took the two fish off the fire. He invited James over to share them. As the two men ate, they talked about the beauty of the lake and the hillsides. Peter said this was a country fit for princes. He winked at James.

Yes, Galilee was beautiful. But even here in the promised land, Satan might come and whisper his lies to my followers.

I called the other disciples. They chattered to one another as they came closer.

While they joined us, I prayed: *Father, help them understand that I must do what the Scriptures say.*

I stood and crossed my arms. The men became quiet.

"I'm heading toward Jerusalem now," I announced. "I will suffer there. The leaders and the priests and the teachers of the law will reject me. They will hand me over to be killed. Then, on the third day, I will rise up from the dead."

My men were shocked. Some stared at me. Others glared into the fire. They were speechless, except for Peter. He pointed a roasting stick in my face, and shouted, "No, Lord! This will never happen to you!"

I answered at once, "Out of my way, Satan!"

Peter dropped the roasting stick. He opened his mouth to argue.

But before he could, I spoke again. "Peter, you're being a stumbling block! You're not thinking God's way; you're thinking your own way."

He was quiet, and dropped the stick.

"Listen, all of you!" I commanded. "If you decide to come with me, you'll have to put aside your own wants and wishes. You'll have to carry your cross every day, and follow me. If you try to save your life, you'll only lose it. But if you lose it for me and my message — you'll be truly alive!"

I stooped over, picked up Peter's stick, and drew crosses in the sand. One by one, the men slipped away to think once more.

I prayed again: *Father, let my brothers learn from my example. Let them learn how to take up their cross. Let me show them how to die for you...*

Glory, Glory

I HAD ASKED Peter and James and John to climb this mountain with me. "We'll pray together up high," I told them, "where the air is clearest and the sun shines brightest."

We came straight up the steepest side, not stopping to rest. They said almost nothing on the way. I knew their hearts were heavy. They couldn't forget what I told them the week before. They were thinking about crosses and death. But they couldn't talk about it.

When we reached the top, we were breathing heavily and our heartbeats were racing. Far below us we could spot the River Jordan and the wide Sea of Galilee and our hometowns nearby. Still, even Peter had nothing to say.

When we caught our breaths, we knelt and bowed our heads. One by one, these three men thanked God for the privilege of being with me and with one another. They asked for God's protection for their families at home. They asked for their daily bread.

Then I began to pray: "My Father, holy is your name. Your kingdom come. Your will be done. And may your glory be shown on earth as it is in heaven...."

Already those three tired men were nodding their heads in drowsiness. Soon their whole bodies were lying on the ground. Their sleep was deep.

A burst of light woke them into alertness, and brought them scrambling to their feet.

They saw me as light — all light. I held out my arms. My body's brightness was so strong I could see it shining right through my clothing.

Then I looked up. My Father had sent down two of our most faithful servants who ever walked on earth.

"Greetings, faithful Moses," I said to the first man. He worshiped me, and asked, "Lord, will you return now to your Father's side?" In answer, I told Moses that before I returned, my Father had work for me to do here.

"Greetings, faithful Elijah," I said to the second man. He worshiped me, and asked, "Lord, what is the work you must do?"

I told Elijah that I must be killed, to take away the sins of the world. "I will destroy sin's power," I said, "by taking all sin upon my sinless body. And I will destroy death, by dying and by rising from the dead after three days. Then I will return to my Father's glory. All this is for you, Elijah, and for everyone. It is my blood that wins a place in heaven for you."

Moses and Elijah bowed again in worship, and sang praises to me.

My disciples with their earthly eyes were still squinting at all the light. They were fearful and

uncertain. Peter tried to speak now, but his words made little sense.

I held out my arms, sending out light rays from my fingertips. I looked up. *My Father,* I prayed, *my disciples believe in me. And because they believed first without seeing my glory, you've let them see it. Now, let them also* hear *my glory.*

A cloud instantly covered the mountain. My Father's voice came as powerful as thunder. We could feel it as well as hear it. The mountain shook beneath our feet. He spoke clear and unhurried, so my disciples could understand every word: "This is my beloved Son," he shouted, "and I delight in him. Listen to him!"

Peter and James and John fell to the ground. They covered their heads with their arms.

Thank you, Father, I quietly prayed. Then there was silence.

After a moment, the men cautiously raised their heads. Moses and Elijah were gone, and my brightness had dimmed. "Don't be afraid," I told them. I put an arm around each man's shoulders as I helped them one by one to their feet.

The air was clear. Down below we could see Galilee and the River Jordan and our home-towns.

I led the way down the mountain. As we stepped carefully along the steep slope and its loose rocks, I said to my disciples, "Tell no one what you saw up there — until I've risen from the dead."

Childlike

⸻⸻❧❧❧⸻⸻

U P IN THE TREE, they giggled and wiggled to see me. I quickly asked these children all their names.

Yesterday my disciples tried to chase them away. But now those men knew better, after I corrected them. Today the men were looking on, smiling and watching to see what I would do.

The children offered a suggestion. They wanted me to come up in the tree with them. "Please?" said the boy named Nathan.

"Sure," I said. "Let me show you my fastest way up." I gathered the bottom of my robe and tucked and tied it, then swung a leg over the lowest branch and scrambled on up. When it came to climbing trees as a boy, I had always been the first and the fastest and the highest. But I would always reach down to help the other children, so they could join me up high. I did it now again.

"Say, what if we wanted to climb higher?" I asked, when we were snuggled at the top. "Could we?"

"No," Nathan said with a smile. "We ran out of tree."

I laughed with him. "You're right," I agreed. "We can't go any higher in this one. But what if you wanted to climb higher than a tree? What if you wanted to climb all the way up to God? What could you do?"

They were quiet, searching their minds for answers.

"Could there be a ladder or a stairway somewhere," I suggested, "with steps going up to heaven?"

Their faces brightened as they remembered the story in Scripture of Jacob's dream. They told me all about it.

"But it was only a dream," Nathan sadly mentioned.

"Yes, it was a dream," I replied, "but a dream about something real. There truly is a stairway to heaven. I myself am that stairway."

"Are you sure?" Nathan asked.

"Yes! And if you believe me, someday soon you'll discover just how right I am."

Each of them nodded trustingly. They knew I would never lie to them, or hurt them.

"Now, let me show you the fastest way down."

I dropped a few branches below, then jumped to the ground. They followed me. I caught them one by one as they fell from the tree, and I gave each one a hug from my Father.

Time to Listen

WITH QUICK MOTIONS, Martha struck her spoon against the side of the bowl. It wasn't a pounding sound— just a *tap, tap, tap*. For our dinner she was preparing lentil soup, a favorite meal of mine.

Her sister Mary didn't notice the noise. In fact, she showed no awareness of Martha even being in the room. For the last hour Mary had been sitting here, soaking up every word I said.

I continued with a story I was telling: "Then the rains came, enough to bring a flood. And a stormwind blew: a fierce gale that battered that man's house—"

Bam! Martha slammed down her spoon. She stomped over to the doorway and snatched a broom from where Mary had left it standing an hour ago. Martha's arms made wide, furious strokes as she swept. It raised a cloud of dust. But her sister's eyes were still on me.

Dear Father, I quickly prayed, *thank you that Mary's eyes truly see and her ears truly hear. Help all my children to know what Mary knows: that when I am speaking, it's time to receive, not to give; that when I am speaking, she serves me best by listening.*

I went back to the story, "But that man's house suffered no damage, Mary, because—"

"Master!" Martha said. She set the broom aside, and put her fists on her hips. She was pouting. "Master, doesn't it bother you that Mary has left all this work to me?"

Mary's attention was broken. She quickly stood, and put her hand to her mouth. She looked at her sister, and at the broom, then back to me.

"Please, Master," Martha went on. "Make her help me."

I understood how Martha felt. She wanted to honor me with a good meal and a tidy house. But how could she know what I really wanted if she didn't listen to me?

"Martha, Martha," I said, "you let so many things worry you and distract you. But really, only one thing is absolutely necessary. Mary has chosen what's best. And I won't take it away from her." Mary saw the approval in my eyes. She sat down again in front of me.

"Martha," I said to her sister, "would you care to hear the rest of the story with Mary?"

Martha threw a quick glance at the soup, then shrugged, and stepped closer to us. She rested her arm on Mary's shoulder, and asked me to start the story again at the beginning.

So I did. "This story will show you," I said, "what the person is like who hears what I say, and puts it into practice..."

Cheers and Tears

I PASSED A BOY with a lamb on his shoulders. I heard his high voice repeating the words that all on the streets of Jerusalem were shouting: "Hosanna! Hosanna to the Son of David!" For a few steps, he kept pace with the donkey I was riding. He thrust his face up close to mine. "You know," the boy said, "I like to pretend I'm David!"

I gently patted the lamb he carried, and gave a shake to the little shepherd's head as well. Onward I rode. The cheering swelled.

But louder to me was a passage from the prophet Zechariah. I let the words sound in my heart: *Look at me! Don't be afraid! See, I'm your king, and I come to you in humbleness, riding a donkey — yes, even the young colt of a donkey.*

Beneath me, the frisky donkey colt pranced ahead, enjoying this commotion. The people shouted the ancient words from the Psalms: "Blessed is he who comes in the name of the Lord!"

Blessed — the word means "happy." Yes, I come in the name of the Lord, and I am blessed. But how many of these people notice the tears in my eyes?

Today they all so willingly praise me. But I won't force them to keep it up, though I am indeed their rightful king. Before this Passover is ended, they'll let Satan have his way. Soon they'll let their leaders turn their hearts against me.

I looked deeply into a face here, and a face there. Yes, only a few days from now, this person and that one will be viciously demanding my death.

I was crying not for me, but for them. Who among them truly saw who I was? Most people in Jerusalem would never understand the peace from God that I came to offer. Therefore, Jerusalem had only war to wait for.

I looked over my shoulder. My disciples were leading the people in more praise and applause. The boy with his lamb was now alongside Peter. His little legs did double-time to keep up with the big fisherman. Tears came again to my eyes. Before this week was over, he too would be screaming against me.

His hero David had known so much about me a thousand years before, without even seeing me. Now this boy had seen me with his own eyes — but he didn't understand.

Our noisy parade came to the approach leading into the temple courts. A Pharisee came out and ran down the steps, waving his fists. "Quiet!" he yelled. "Order, order!" The crowd took no notice. So he called out to me, "Teacher, won't you control this mob?"

But my Father had made today a day of praise. "No, I won't," I answered the Pharisee. "Besides, if I kept these people quiet, the walls would do the shouting today!"

No, I would not stop these voices now from shouting "Hosanna!" — just as I would not stop them later from yelling, "Crucify!"

Hatred

W ITH CONFIDENT STEPS the men made their way through the busy temple courts. Every one of them wore a long robe of the best cloth. Each man was looking at me. And each one wore a smile.

I knew them. I knew they were all liars. I knew they were tricksters. I knew each one had a wicked heart. I saw all their sin at once, and I hated the ugliness and dirtiness of it. How I detested it!

My father and I created these men in our own image. We gave them breath and heartbeats so they could love us, and teach their families and neighbors about us. We gave them food each day, and clothing. We gave them the Scriptures, and we gave them their minds and their hearts to understand and obey the Scriptures. We gave them all they needed to do right.

But instead they hated me, just as they hated my Father. They wanted to trap me. Their plan was to get me to speak against the Roman government. They would report my rebellious words, so the Romans would arrest me.

They stopped in front of me. Their leader's smile was only half an arm's length from my face. From every corner of the temple courts, other people crowded around to see what this was about.

"Teacher," the leader said, with a little bow, "you're a good teacher, so honest, so fair. Now give us your help with a question we have. What do you think: Is it right to give taxes to the Romans? Should we pay, or not?"

I looked again into each man's face, knowing each man's heart. "Why are you hypocrites trying to trick me?" I asked. I saw a slight twitch in the leader's smile.

I thrust out my hand, palm upward, at his chest. "Show me the coin that's used to pay the tax," I asked.

His smile went away. He raised his arm and nervously snapped his fingers. "Somebody get one!" he mumbled to his partners.

The others began fumbling under the flowing folds of their robes. Here and there a purse came out, and a few coins glinted in the sunlight. Finally someone passed a denarius to the leader, who was snapping his fingers again.

He took the coin in his upraised hand. Slowly he lowered it to place the money in my palm.

"Who is this?" I said at once. "Whose picture is it?"

As if he didn't know, he looked down at the denarius. It was resting in my hand — in the hand from which all true riches flow, and the hand into which all things must one day be returned.

The leader looked up. "Caesar's," he acknowledged.

I grabbed his hand, and slapped the coin into it.

"Then give Caesar what is Caesar's," I commanded. "And give God what is God's."

I felt his fingers grip the coin, then he jerked his hand away.

His face showed only shock. He and the men with him cautiously stepped back, still staring at me, unable to speak.

Finally the leader mumbled, and tucked the coin inside his robe. He turned with the others to hurry out.

After parting to make way for the men, the crowd looked back at me. And they broke out in applause and cheers.

Everything

I SAT DOWN on the stone floor of the temple court. I rested my back against a column. Again this morning, as I had every morning this week, I came to the temple and taught the crowds. For their own good I told them what my Father told me to say.

I was a light shining in a dark place, like a torch inside a tomb. I showed these people their sins. They were greedy. They were boastful. They were selfish, and cruel, and dishonest.

I showed them all that. But they didn't want to change.

Now there was nothing more I could tell them until the Judgment Day.

I turned to the right, to the place where people put money in the temple treasury. A woman was there. She was a widow. She dropped in two coins that together were worth less than a penny. I knew at once that she had no other money to her name. She might have kept one coin for herself. But she didn't. She gave everything.

I would remember her gift on the Judgment Day.

"Quick! Come and look," I said to my disciples nearby. They gathered close, and I nodded toward the woman.

"She gave more than those rich men did," I said, "because she gave everything."

The woman walked away, out of sight.

Now it was my turn. The time had come for me to give everything. I could keep a part of my life for myself, but I would not. I would give my all. And even then — even when I had given all, and had nothing left — I would still be giving. By becoming poor, I would make others rich.

"Let's go," I told my disciples.

They followed as I walked out of the temple for the very last time.

A Last Meal

EVERYTHING WAS READY. Peter and John had seen to that, just as I asked them to. Stepping into this upstairs room, I even saw the wash basin and towel. It was ready for cleaning the dust and dung of the streets off our feet before we ate.

Peter saw me admiring everything. He beamed with pleasure, and wiped his hands on his clothes.

The other disciples stepped in behind me. The aroma of roast lamb and other food met us at the doorway. The men hurried around me to take their places at the table.

They ignored the wash basin and towel.

This would be my last meal with these twelve men before everything changed. How eagerly I looked forward to this time!

"Master," Peter said, "would you give thanks for us now?"

I left the towel and basin, and sat at the table with them. I gave thanks to my Father for this meal, and for everything it meant. I gave thanks for the men I loved who would share it with me.

"Amen."

The bowls of food immediately began circling the table, and hungry hands reached in.

James was on my left. His feet weren't far from my face. From the way they smelled and looked, he must have stepped in a fresh pile of donkey manure on his way in. Next to James was Peter. His wrinkled nose told me that he smelled them, too. But Peter made no move for the wash water.

On my right was John. Judas was next to him, and his feet were filthy, too. John's frown told me he had noticed. But John stayed put, saying nothing. Then I saw that John's feet were almost as grubby as Judas's.

I got up, and stepped away from the table. I took off my robe, and wrapped the towel around my waist. I put the basin of water on the floor beside John. I untied his left sandal, and I did for him what I would gladly do for anyone. I took this fisherman's foot in my hand, lapped water on it, and rubbed off the dirt with my fingers, from heel to toes.

I silently prayed. *Thank you, Father, for giving me this man John, whom I truly love.*

All twelve men had stopped eating. They were so quiet, it seemed they had stopped breathing as well.

After I washed John's other foot, I moved on to the man beside him. I prayed: *Thank you, Father, for Judas, whom I have truly loved and served.*

As I scrubbed his ankles, I closed my eyes in sorrow. These were feet my Father and I had made. But tonight they would take Judas where Satan wanted him to go.

I crossed over to Peter. I saw him turning his feet this way and that, to check them. They looked a little cleaner than usual.

I set the basin right beside him.

"But Lord," he objected, "you aren't doing mine, are you?"

"Right now you don't understand what I'm doing," I explained. "Later you will."

He bent his knees to draw his feet up close. "No. I can't let you do it," he insisted. "Never!"

Silently I asked my Father to open Peter's heart. *Help him see how much I love him. Help him see how much he needs to let my love wash him all over, inside and out.*

"If I don't wash you," I told Peter, "you have nothing to do with me."

Peter watched me cup my hands and lower them into the water. A flash of understanding came to his eyes.

He quickly stretched out his feet. "Then do my hands and my head, too," he said.

I grinned. "You've had a bath," I reminded him. "Only your feet are dirty."

Thank you, Lord, for Peter and the others here who have heard my words, and believed me. I'm glad to clean them! Soon I will clean their hearts with my blood — and my blood cleans whiter than snow.

A Last Request

FOR THE THIRD TIME I slowly made my way back to Peter and James and John. For the third time, I found them sleeping, though I had asked them to stay awake and pray. Above me, the wind rustled the leaves on the twisty branches of the olive trees. Nearby I heard the sad, sweet calling of a dove.

My eyes were burning and blurry. Through my tears, I could see one of the city gates across the moonlit valley. I saw a large crowd there, carrying torches.

They were coming.

I looked up through the swaying olive branches, and cried out, "I trust you, Father! But how I'll miss your smile shining down on me! How I'll miss your voice calling out your love!"

I felt my knees weaken. I fell to the ground again, and leaned my arms on a rock.

"O Father! You know I've perfectly loved you and obeyed you and known you. Dear Father, I know everything is possible with you. I ask you again, if there's any other way — if I can do this work without going away from you, then let it be. Father, I want to be with you, and nowhere else! But even more I want to do whatever you say is right. I'll do everything you ask. Your will be done."

I closed my eyes. My Father spoke again to me. Once more he told me his plan: "I love the world so much, that I will give up my only Son..."

His voice was as gentle and tender as ever, and as strong and fatherly as ever. Tonight its music was a thousand times sweeter, because I knew that soon I wouldn't be able to hear it.

I dropped my forehead on my hands. I felt my warm tears flowing like blood down my wrists. And I felt my Father's love for every man and woman and boy and girl that we had made.

I heard voices. The crowd with torches was closer. I raised my head. The breeze had stopped. The trees were still. The dove no longer sang.

I stood, and stepped over to nudge Peter and James and John. "Wake up," I told them. "Look! The traitor is coming."

Alone

I WOULD NOT stop them. "Here I am!" I shouted, stepping out in front of my disciples.

Judas had come first, greeting me with a kiss. With that signal, the arresting mob had hurried forward. Judas stepped back to stand with them.

They made a wall in front of us. Some carried swords. Some carried clubs. I heard several men breathing heavily.

They held their torches high. Sparks flew upward through the tree limbs. The wall of men

stood, but came no closer, though I knew they could all see me clearly.

"Who is it you want?" I asked.

On Judas's right, a man answered, "Jesus of Nazareth!"

"Here I am!" I called out again. The words seemed to scare them. Several men took a step back. The wall was wavering.

Above the trees, I could hear a low hum — the sound of demons' wings.

I took a step closer. "I told you who I am. If you're after me, let these others go." I pointed to my disciples behind me.

The drone of the demons sounded louder. Cautiously, the armed men in the mob began stepping forward. I made no move to stop them. Slowly, the wall closed in.

Behind me I heard murmuring. I turned to look. Peter was rushing forward to fight, waving a sword above his head, with both hands on the handle. He let his weapon strike in the midst of the crowd, then rushed to my side and grabbed my shoulder. The men in the mob raised their clubs and swords to strike back. One man groaned and fell to his knees, clutching his ear with both hands. Blood was dripping through his fingers.

I rebuked Peter at once. "Enough of this!" I shouted. Both sides held their peace.

I reached down and touched the wounded man. I gently pulled back his hands from the side of his face. His ear was healed. The blood was gone, even from his fingers.

I turned again to Peter and the other disciples, who had closed in behind him. "Put the sword away," I commanded. "Don't you understand? Even now I could call my Father and he would send me twelve armies of angels."

Every man there was holding his breath. Even the demons were silent.

"But the Scriptures have said it must happen this way," I continued quietly. "I will drink the cup my Father gave me."

I held out my arms to the mob. "So you've come out to capture me with swords and clubs, have you — as if I were a robber? I've been teaching in the temple every day, and you didn't take me then! But now — this is your hour! Now is the time for darkness to have all the power!"

Above the trees, I heard the shriek and squeal of the evil spirits.

The men in the mob put aside all their caution and fear. They jerked my arms to pull me forward. Others closed in behind and shoved me by my neck and shoulders.

I looked back once. I saw Peter drop the sword, as he and my other disciples ran away into the darkness.

Lies

⟨⟨⟨⟨

THEY HAD SLAPPED ME once, lightly. And they had pushed and shoved me. But now that all the religious leaders had gathered here, they were going after me only with words.

I heard them lie again and again, accusing me of this and that. They wanted to have me killed, and they needed a reason.

As each man spoke his lying words, I looked into his eyes. I made no answer to any charge. I kept my lips closed.

Once I glanced down at my arms hanging before me. My wrists were throbbing. They were bound too tightly with a leather cord. My fingers were becoming numb.

The high priest rose from his chair. His face was full of angry wrinkles. "Do you refuse to answer these charges?" he barked.

I said nothing.

Behind him, some of the leaders coughed uncomfortably. They squirmed in their chairs. As they stared at me, I saw them rubbing their bearded chins, or squinting their eyes.

I saw the high priest's anger boiling up because of my silence. He had not expected this. He wanted to quarrel with me, just as all men want to quarrel with God. Yes, there's a raging quarrel between God and men. It's a terrible disagreement. But one side is all wrong, and the other is perfectly right. All the blame belongs to the people. None of the blame belongs to God.

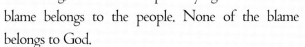

So there is no way any human being can win this argument. No one can ever patch things up with the living, holy God. Only God himself could fix the problem.

And that was why I was here.

I heard a few demons in the top of the room, buzzing like flies.

The high priest slowly raised his hand to point at me. His finger was shaking. His voice trembled as well.

"I charge you under oath, by the living God," he uttered. "Are you the Messiah? Are you the Son of God?"

I stared into his dark eyes, and opened my mouth. "It's just as you say. I am."

Every man in the room let out a gasp. I saw a flash of delight on the face of the high priest. He had found his reason to kill me. He turned to the other men. But I spoke to them first, for I could see the future. I let my voice ring out in every corner of that stuffy room: "I tell you all, you will see me in power sitting at God's right hand! And I'll come back to earth on the clouds of heaven."

The high priest staggered back. He grabbed the arms of his chair to steady himself.

As he straightened up, still glaring at me, he threw both hands to his chest. He clutched the front collar of his inner robe. His knuckles were white, and his teeth clenched. He yanked with all his might. The robe ripped loudly down the front, to below his waist, as his arms spread wide.

"You have heard him yourselves!" he cried to the others. "You heard what he dared to say! What is your judgment?"

The leaders rushed to their feet. "He deserves to die!" one yelled. The others roared their approval. They jerked their fists and fingers at me. "Death!" they shouted. "Death! *Death!*"

Their screams mingled into one sound with the hooting of the demons above them.

I saw the high priest glancing beyond me, signaling with his hand. Behind me I heard the tromping of the temple soldiers who had guarded the doorway. They stopped on each side of me, and squeezed my arms.

Still shouting, still punching the air with their fists, the leaders stepped forward to encircle me. Then one of them spit at me. I held my head high, and turned my other cheek toward him. Another man spit at me, then another, and another. Behind me, the men began beating my back with their fists. Others jerked on my beard and my hair.

I closed my eyes. *Help me now, Father,* I pleaded. *Help me show how to stay strong. I've always trusted you, and I trust you now. Whatever these men do to me, I know that you are allowing it, so I can finish what you want me to do. I trust you, O Father. I trust you!*

"Come with me!" a soldier behind me shouted.

I opened my eyes and turned to obey, just as if the order had been spoken by my Father.

Crucify!

IT WAS MORNING of the day I would die. But the sunlight hurt my eyes.

Whenever I opened them, I had to blink and lean back my head to keep out the blood. It trickled down from where a crown of thorns had been smashed into my head. I could feel where it had punctured my scalp all around, and through the skin on my forehead. My head throbbed with pain.

The never-ending noise made it even worse. The crowd at the Roman palace and the demons above them were roaring. I closed my eyes.

"Look at your king!" I heard Pilate say.

Below him, the people continued their screams: "Crucify! Crucify!"

"But he's your king!" Pilate shouted.

"Away with him!" they shouted back. "We have no king but Caesar!" Still louder they thundered: "Crucify! Crucify! Crucify!..."

I opened my eyes and blinked away the blood. I saw Pilate nod.

A servant brought him a wash basin. Pilate dipped in his hands and washed them. "You all see it," he proclaimed. "I'm innocent of this man's blood!"

No, I thought, *you are not. No one is innocent of my blood. Either a man is for God, or against him. And everyone has turned against him. Everyone has gone his own way.*

Pilate turned his back to the clamor of the crowd. He signaled to the soldiers behind me. I barely heard his voice above the crowd. "Take him," he ordered, "and crucify him."

Today with Me

ALL MY BODY was burning with pain. I felt the fire shooting from my wrists through my shoulders. It shot up from my feet into my legs and thighs, and along my back where the whip lashes had fallen. With the slightest turn of my face, a flame of pain flashed across my eyes. The hottest fire was in my chest, where my lungs wanted to explode with every breath.

I felt my strength melting away from all this heat inside my dying body.

I knew it would be this way. Long ago I had understood the words in the Twenty-second Psalm that told me how I would feel: *I am poured out like water... My heart has turned to wax, melting away within me... They have pierced my hands and my feet....*

But now I felt something worse than the burning. It was like a great weight falling all over me, squeezing in from every side. I felt it pounding my head, blinding my eyes, and ramming my shoulders and chest. It was slowly crushing me. It was sin — all the sin, of all the world. It was all the wrong things that every man or woman or boy or girl had ever done, for all time. It brought a far worse hurt to me than any human being could ever bear.

This, too, I had known was coming. I remembered more words about me, words that my Father had given to Isaiah: *He was crushed for our sins.... It was the Lord's will to crush him...*

The pain was made worse by the noise blasting my ears. Below me, people kept daring me to come down. Above their shouts I heard demons screaming in wild delight, stirring up the crowd, making them crazy with anger. They sounded like wild beasts, just as the Twenty-second

Psalm had said: *Many bulls surround me on every side.... Roaring lions open their mouths against me....*

I could hardly hear my Father's voice in the Scriptures anymore. The attack of sin was blocking out the song of Scripture from my mind and heart. My Father's words in my Father's voice had been my greatest joy all my life, like a constant friend who never left me. But now God was turning his back on his Son.

In horrible grief, I looked up. The sky was so thick with demons now that they shut out all light from heaven. Day was like night.

I heard another raging noise. It came from the man being crucified on my left. I took another burning breath. I held it, trying to listen above the crowd. He was yelling at me. "Don't you hear?" he said. "Save yourself and us, if you're the Messiah!"

I took another breath. Another painful flame exploded in my lungs. No, I would not save myself, even though I could. But yes, I was doing everything to save him. I was giving my all.

Now I heard another voice. The man being crucified on my right was shouting, too — but not at me. He was scolding the other prisoner: "We're getting only what we deserve! But this man never did anything wrong."

In slow agony I turned my head to the right. I opened my burning eyes. At the end of my arm, at the tip of my fingers, I saw this man facing me on the other cross.

Suddenly a blow came slamming into my head and shoulders and chest. It was the same dark, crushing weight as before, but it was even heavier now. I knew that this time the crashing weight included every sin of this man on my right — and his sins were many. I closed my eyes and let it all come pounding down on me. I heard the demons scream even louder.

Then came another bruising blow, then another, and another, and another. Each wave of sin that crashed over me was harder and heavier than the last. I silently prayed: "How long, O Lord? How long?" But there was no answer. My Father's voice was silent.

I fought to reopen my eyes. The man was still looking at me. At once, even with all the pain, I saw the faith in his face. That one look to me was like cool rain on this awful day of fire.

"Jesus," the man said. "Remember me when you come into your kingdom."

Now there was no break from the battering waves of sin and death. The demons roared. I let the storm keep coming. Soon the crushing would be complete. Soon I would drop into total darkness. But for a fleeting moment, I saw a ray of joy shining beyond the black. I caught a glimpse of this man's face far away, in the light of my Father's home. There was a bright circle of other faces, too: men and women, girls and boys. Then the picture blacked out.

I took another breath, with another explosion of pain. I tried to swallow, but my mouth and throat were dry. It hurt even to part my lips, but I wanted to speak to this man now.

"Today," I said — my voice was a raspy whisper — "today, you'll be with me in Paradise."

Morning

I HEARD THE FIRST morning music of the sparrows, singing as cheerfully as ever. And I heard a woman weeping. Mary Magdalene was on her knees by the grave where my body was lying until a few hours ago.

I remembered when seven demons lived inside Mary, and kept her sad and bitter and cranky. Back then she stayed up all night to be in the darkness, and she slept during the day.

Then I cast the demons out. Right away she started loving the mornings. She was always up before dawn. Songbirds and sunrise and sparkling morning dew became her favorite treasures.

But today she didn't hear the birds or notice the dew. Her heart was too broken. She was even wondering if she would always have to be sad and bitter and cranky again.

But I rejoiced over Mary. *Thank you, Father, for the joy she'll know in just a moment. Thank you for letting me die for her and for all who believe in me, so they can live a new life and be clean, and come to heaven soon and worship you forever.*

I stepped toward her. "Why are you weeping?" I asked.

She glanced over her shoulder. She could hardly see me through her tears. She held her face in her hands as she answered: "They've taken away my Lord, and I don't know where!"

"Who are you looking for?" I asked.

She had assumed I was simply the caretaker of this garden. Now she wondered what I knew about the empty tomb. "Sir, if you took him, please tell me where you laid him."

Father, I prayed, *open her eyes and her ears and her heart...*

"Mary," I said.

She knew the voice instantly. "Dear Teacher!" she exclaimed, and now she was crying again, this time for joy. She rushed closer to fall at my feet. She would gladly have held on to me and gazed at me forever. But that must wait for heaven.

First I had work for her to do, as I always have for those who come to me. I asked her to tell my disciples that she had seen me, and that I would soon be going home to heaven.

She listened carefully. In quick obedience she rose to go, and at the same time noticed the songs of the sparrows.

She had already become a much better Mary than before. And she would become even better.

As she left the garden, I held out my wounded arms, and looked to the sky. *Thank you, Father, that I can wear these scars forever, so that Mary and all my children won't have to wear theirs. They live here on the earth where the devil roams about and roars like a lion. But when they come home to us in heaven, they'll be like Daniel, who didn't have even a scratch when he came out from the lions' den. In the same way, your children will be perfect when they're carried up from earth to heaven.*

I watched Mary hurry down the path to the city. She held her face high and her hands high. She was drinking in the morning sun, and singing.

On Fire

T HE TWO MEN were walking fast and talking fast. But they stopped when I came up behind them. They turned frightened faces toward me.

Their names were Cleopas and Lucas. Both had heard me teach many times, and both believed. But I didn't let them recognize me now. First I needed to light a flame in their hearts.

I laid my arms on their shoulders and stepped ahead, to encourage them to keep going.

"What were you discussing just now?" I asked. I would let them speak first, so they would listen more later. We were on the seven-mile road from Jerusalem to Emmaus, and the journey was far enough for a long conversation.

"What else," answered Cleopas, "except for all the things happening in Jerusalem?"

"What things?" I asked.

He wondered if I was a newly arrived stranger, not to have heard about the man Jesus. "He was so strong in everything he did and said," Cleopas declared. "We were sure he was Christ our Savior. But three days ago our leaders arrested him and had him crucified."

Lucas shook his head while Cleopas sadly continued: "On top of all that, there was a rumor this morning that Jesus is alive. So some of our men went to his tomb. They found it empty, all right. But they didn't see Jesus."

Cleopas and Lucas were honest with me. Now I would be honest with them.

"How foolish you are!" I stated. They jerked their heads in surprise. "You aren't believing the Scriptures," I continued. "The prophets make it clear that Christ would have to suffer."

I told them that Christ is everywhere in the Scriptures, in all the words on every scroll. Then I proved it to them. Over the next half-dozen miles, I carefully explained God's Word to them, and everything it said about me. They listened and their gloom disappeared. A brightness in their eyes told me that a spark was growing and glowing inside them.

The sun was setting as we entered Emmaus. At the door where they were staying, they begged me to come in and be their guest. I was delighted. When my Father and I give good things to our children, we're always eager to hear them ask for more.

Inside we sat down for bread. They put me at the head of the table. When I pulled up my sleeves and held up the bread to break it, they saw my scars from the nails.

Their jaws dropped. Their eyes widened. Yes, they believed: This was their Lord!

My work with them today was done. I vanished from their sight. They couldn't see me, but I saw Cleopas stand and clutch his chest and say, "Lucas, didn't your heart burn inside you while he opened up the Scriptures to us?"

I left them, and prayed, *Father, help them remember that the way to have a heart on fire is to keep seeing me in your Word.*

Home

S OON I WOULD BE THERE. Soon I would be wrapped in my Father's welcoming arms. I would leave the world below. I would live above, where everything is always goodness and always light.

I would be at my Father's side, and my Father himself is goodness and light, and he is always the same, yesterday and today and forever. I am his Son, and I too am always the same, yesterday and today and forever.

I felt a breeze tossing my hair and rippling my white robe. I was higher than a snowy mountaintop, but the breeze was warm, and it smelled like home.

From far away, I heard a song my Father and I had taught the angels before the beginning of time. I looked up. A cloud was rolling down quickly to meet me in the air.

I gazed once more at the hillside growing smaller beneath my feet. My disciples were reaching up, longing for me. I stretched out my hands to bless them.

Father, their hearts are clean now, like a new scroll with nothing written on it. I myself have washed them with my blood, and my blood cleans whiter than snow. When you look at them, my Father, look first at me and remember the price we paid to win them.

Father, I've left them in the world. Protect them from the evil one, until the day comes when I destroy him forever.

But I've promised not to leave my disciples alone in the world. Father, send our Holy Spirit to write your law of love on their hearts. Send our Holy Spirit to protect them, and to keep them clean, and to keep them busy and happy at my work.

Higher I rose. The angel song grew louder. It was coming from thousands of voices. I recognized each one. Their song came to a mighty end, with trumpets and bells and cymbals.

There was silence as the cloud enfolded me. It wasn't wet and foggy and cold, like earthly clouds, but warm and bright. Inside it, I could see everything forever. I looked down and could see all the world for all of history. I could see all the universe my Father and I created — every star in every galaxy, every spark in every fire, every atom in every molecule. I could see all of it, all at once, forever.

And right above me — opening high and wide all around — I saw all of heaven, and the One who fills it with himself.

"Father!" I cried. "Father! I'm home!..."

Today

I SEE YOU. Right now I'm looking at you, and I always see you, every moment. I see every step you take. I see everything you hold in your hand. I see every thought you have in your mind.

I know you. I know all about you. I knew it all before you were even born. Before you took your first breath, I knew what would happen on every day of your life.

I know all your secrets. I know all your plans. I know everything you wish for and hope for. I know what makes you happy.

I know everything you're afraid of. I know everything you're worried about. I know your every hurt. I know what makes you angry. I know what makes you sad.

I see you. I know you. And I love you.

When I lived on earth, *Immanuel* was one of the names my Father gave me. It means, "God with us." I came to earth just to be *with* you.

I was with you especially when I died on the cross. And you were with me, because in my body I took on every wrong thing you ever did. Every sin you ever committed was a part of me then. Every lie you ever told, every angry word you ever spoke, every mean or mocking thought you ever had, was a part of me. Yes, I was with you, and you were with me.

I was with you even more when I rose up from the dead. You were with me when I proved that I'm more powerful than sin and death. You also are more powerful than sin and death, by believing in me and letting the world know you believe.

Death isn't in Satan's hands anymore. It's in my hands. So you have nothing to fear. Instead of being the gateway to pain and torture in hell, death will be your doorway to heaven, where there is no more pain or crying or sickness.

Here in my Father's home is a place I'm preparing just for you, where you can stay with me. It's a perfectly safe place, and it's perfectly thrilling too. Heaven is bigger and wider and higher and faster and brighter and louder and more fun than all the exciting places in your world put together.

You'll see me as clearly then as I can see you now. We'll always be together, and my love will never stop surprising you. Yes, this place is just right for you. I know it's a perfect match, because I see you, and I know you, and I love you.

You'll be here soon. While you wait, I'm praying for you. I never stop praying for you, because I always know what you need and I care for you.

I love you. And because I love you, I know you. And because I know you — I will never let you out of my sight.